CHASE THE WIND

Dorian Petersen Potter

CHASE THE WIND

I want to dedicate this poetry book to God, and to Jesus Christ,
my Lord and my Savior. They had always been in my life
the biggest and greatest inspiration of all.
Thank You God and Jesus for all that You both had
done, and for your most wonderful gift of
love, forgiveness and salvation.

For So Long

(Sonnet)

How I long for days when my heart was free
When often dreams brought lots of smiles and glee
Remember today all your kisses again
With excitement that always dwells in.
Holding my pen I'm ready again to write,
Say bye to this day and welcomed the night.
Tell me how could I ever be so wrong?
When I've loved you with passion for so long
Hope and devotion pieces chards of my heart
But with each beat you take it all apart.
And time seems to stand all of sudden still
With crafty words and lies, love, turns hearts ill.
How I long for days care-free of youth when
We walked so in love hand in hand, back then.

*
*

~Today And Forever~
(Quatern)

Without God don't know where I'd be
He sends blessings that's clear to see
He gives love today forever
Grants forgiveness and leaves never.

No matter what He sees thru all
Without God don't know where I'd be
There are days it's hard to stand tall
He sends blessings that's clear to see.

No matter what He sees thru all
With Jesus thru things I can go
Without God don't know where I'd be
With his divine love each day grow.

He gives love today forever
He sends blessings that's clear to see
Grants forgiveness and leaves never
Without God don't know where I'd be.

~SHINING~
(KYRIELLE SONNET)

**STAY FOCUS TILL YOU REACH YOUR GOAL
TAKE IT SLOW AND WATCH FOR YOUR SOUL
DON'T RUSH AND YOU WILL BE JUST FINE
KNOW WITH GOD'S LOVE AND HELP YOU'LL SHINE**

**STAY FOCUS IN YOUR HEART AND MIND
DO YOUR PART REMEMBER GOD'S KIND
AS HE HAS YOUR HEART IN A SHRINE
KNOW WITH GOD'S LOVE AND HELP YOU'LL SHINE**

**GOD FOR SURE HAS A PLAN FOR YOU
AND ALWAYS SHOWS ALL HIS LOVE TRUE
IF YOU LET HIM YOU'LL WALK THE LINE
KNOW WITH GOD'S LOVE AND HELP YOU'LL SHINE**

**STAY FOCUS TILL YOU REACH YOUR GOAL
KNOW WITH GOD'S LOVE AND HELP YOU'LL SHINE**

*

*

~CHANGES~
(DOUBLE TAKE 6'S 5'S AND 4'S)

PRAY FOR LOVE PEACE TODAY
LOVE COMES FROM LORD SEE
HE WILL SET YOU FREE
HELP YOU EACH SINGLE DAY

HE'LL CHANGE YOUR HEART
AND HOLD YOUR HAND
BE MORE HAPPY
WITH HIM CAN FLY
YOU'LL REJOICE

WITH GOD YOU OBTAIN PEACE
THINGS BETTER YOU KNOW
WHEN TROUBLE STIR SO
WITH HIM YOU CAN WIN RACE

HE'LL CHANGE YOUR HEART
AND HOLD YOUR HAND
SING SONG EACH DAY
PRAISE HIS NAME TOO
HIS TEACHINGS NICE

*

*

~FIRST~
(SKELETON KEY)

PUT
GODFIRST**
IN
ALL THAT
I JUST DO
HE HAS A PLAN
FOR ME AND YOU EACH MAN
FOLLOW YOUR DREAMS AND TAKE A STAND
GONE ARE THE GOOD OLD DAYS AND LOVE NEEDS THE LAND
TODAY THANK HIM WITH ALL MY HEART
HEALS WHEN THINGS FALL APART
FROM ME HE'LL NEVER PART
HEART WITH HIM SINGS
HE BRINGS
HIS LIGHT
SO BRIGHT
HIS LOVE
THE BEST
WITH HIM
CAN BE
JUST ME
ALL SINS
FORGIVES
IN HIM
I'M FREE
BLESSINGS
TO ME
AND YOU
HE SENDS

~AUTUMN NOTION~
(PICTURE FRAME)

A U T U M N

UNSPEAKABLE VIEW SEEN SO

THE LEAVES FALL DAY NIGHT

UNDER SKY GEESE FLY AND I

MELT UNDER AUTUMN MONO

N O T I O N

*

*

~MOSTLY BAD NEWS~
(FREE STYLE)

ALL OVER THE WORLD I HEAR,
MOSTLY BAD NEWS NEAR AND FAR,
THIS IS TRULY, REALLY BAD,
AND IT MAKES ME VERY SAD.

IT SEEMS THE MEDIA ENJOYS IT,
LOVE TO EXAGERATE IT A BIT;
THEY GIVE US ONLY BAD NEWS,
THINGS THAT MAKES US ALL BLUE.

ALL OVER THE WORLD THERE'S AN ACHE,
BAD NEWS IS WHAT MOST OF US HEAR,
THEY FORGET TO TELL US GOOD NEWS,
AND IT GRIEVE US AND THAT'S CLEAR.

*

*

~AN AFFAIR TO REMEMBER~
(QUATRAINS)

BROUGHT TO YOU WITH LOVE TODAY,
LOOKING DOWN WITH SUCH DELIGHT,
KEEPING YOU HAPPY DAY BY DAY
AS THE MOON ABOVE WATCH US BY

ENTERTAINING YOU ALL THE WAY,
WHAT A DUET WE BOTH MAKE,
KEEPING YOU EVERYDAY IN MY PRAYERS,
BRUSHING WITH BRIGHT COLOR SKIES OF GRAY

LOOKING DOWN WITH SUCH DELIGHT,
IN THIS SACRED TIME OF THE DAY,
WATCHING THE BIRDS BURST IN FLIGHT,
TILL THEY FADE AWAY OUT OF SIGHT

WATER MAKING MAGIC ON THE SHORE,
A QUIET RESPITE FOR US IN THIS PLACE,
EVERYWHERE GRACE SEEMS TO POUR,
COMTEMPLATING MY LOVE YOUR FACE

HEART AND SOUL CAN FLY AWAY,
WHERE LOVE FILL US WITH A GLOW,
WHERE WE CAN SEE RAINBOWS EVERYDAY,
AND OUR MUTUAL LOVE CAN MORE GROW!

*

*

~NO MATTER WHAT~
(DAVEDA'S CASCADE)

**SO HAPPY MY SOUL YOU DID SAVE
TO SIN I DON'T HAVE TO BE SLAVE
MY HEART IN GOD I CAN CONFIDE
LORD YOU ARE MY LIGHT AND MY GUIDE**

**YOU ALWAYS GIVE ME LOVE AND JOY
COMFORT SOUL WHEN I FEEL ANNOY
YOU'LL BE WITH ME BEYOND THE GRAVE
SO HAPPY MY SOUL YOU DID SAVE**

**NO MATTER WHAT TAKES PLACE EACH DAY
IN HIM I CAN HAVE A FRIEND TOO
NONE SHOULD FEAR,SOUL YOU DID SAVE
TO SIN I DON'T HAVE TO BE SLAVE**

**I KNOW THAT WITH HIM I WILL SHINE
I DON'T RUSH I WILL BE JUST FINE
WITH HIM I CAN TAKE THINGS IN STRIDE
MY HEART IN GOD I CAN CONFIDE**

**REMAIN FOCUS IN HEART AND MIND
DO MY PART KNOWING THAT GODS KIND
NOTHING FROM HIM CAN EVER HIDE
LORD YOU ARE MY LIGHT AND MY GUIDE.**

*

*

~ANYDAY ~
(RHYMING COUPLETS)

DON'T PUSH AWAY OR KILL ANY OF YOUR DREAMS TODAY OR ANYDAY.
LIFE'S TOO SHORT SO DONT WASTE IT AND THROW IT ALL AWAY.
LISTEN TO THE RHYTHMS AND THE MUSIC INSIDE YOUR HEART.
THERE'LL BE MUSIC TILL THINGS MAY START TO FALL FOR YOU APART.
TODAY IT MAY BE ME BUT TOMORROW IT MAY BE ALSO THEM OR YOU.
CRUEL WORDS CAN REALLY HURT AND MAKE US ALL SOMETIMES OH SO BLUE.
FEELINGS AND EMOTIONS ARE NOT SOME THAT ONE DAY IN YOU OR ME JUST GREW.
THEY HAVE BEEN THERE AS PART OF YOU AND ME ALWAYS WILL BE THEY'RE NOT NEW.
WITH FAITH AND STRENGH WE CAN ADVANCE FORTH AND MAKE WITH WORK OUR LITTLE WAY.
DURING YOUR JOURNEY YOU'LL FALL SOMETIMES BUT HAVE TO GET UP AND WALK TALL TOO.
PEOPLE,LIFE AND THINGS ARE NOT LIKE THEY MAY SEEM SOMETIMES ALWAYS TO BE.
YOU CAN DO IT ALL,EVERYTHING IT IS POSSIBLE,IF YOU ONLY DARE TO DREAM IT AND SEE.

*

*

~EVERY DAY~
(THE MINUET)

YOU CAN ALWAYS SPREAD HIS LOVE TO
TO ALL AROUND
AROUND BRING JOY
JOY AND LOVE SHOW

LOVE HEALS THE ACHING HEART THAT HURTS
HURTS MAKE LOVE STRONG
STRONG GOD WILL MAKE
MAKE YOU EACH DAY

OBEY GOD SEEK HIS KINGDOM FIRST
FIRST EVERY DAY
DAY WITH PRAYERS
PRAYERS AND SONGS

*

*

~FALL~
(ACROSTIC)

F ANTASTIC COLOURS TO VIEW
A UTUMN IS SO SWIFTLY APPROACHING
L IGHT BRIGHT AND COOL, TREES CHANGE
L EAVES TURN TO REDS,YELLOWS AND BROWNS.

~MAY GOD~
(ANAPHORA)

MAY GOD ALWAYS CARE FOR YOU
MAY GOD KEEP YOU STANDING TALL
MAY GOD WHISPER IN YOUR EARS WORDS OF WISDOM
MAY GOD SHOW YOU WHAT YOU NEED TO KNOW
MAY GOD ALWAYS HAVE AN ANGEL FOR YOU
MAY GOD SEND AN ANGEL BY YOUR SIDE
MAY GOD BE THERE TO CATCH YOU FAST EVERY TIME YOU FALL
MAY GOD GIVE YOU SOMEONE WONDERFUL TO LOVE
MAY GOD TEACH YOU LOVE UNTOLD
MAY GOD GIVE YOU HOPES TO KEEP YOU SAFE AND WARM
MAY GOD GRANT YOU WITH MANY GIFTS AND LONG LIFE
MAY GOD KEEP HIS EYES ALWAYS ON YOU
MAY GOD GUIDE EVERY SINGLE STEP OF YOUR WAY
MAY GOD KEEP YOU FROM EACH AND ALL HARM EACH DAY
MAY GOD ALWAYS SEND AN ANGEL BESIDE YOU
MAY GOD ALWAYS SPEAK TO YOUR HEART MIND AND SOUL.

*

*

~MY HEART~
(JESUS TEARS)

MY
HEART EACH
DAY LEAPS WITH
JOY IN THE LORD
HE WANTS ME TO WALK
ETERNALLY WITH
HIM STRAIGHT ALL
THE WAY
THROUGH

I
DO MAKE
MISTAKES BUT
HE FORGIVES ME
SEE GOD WHEN SUN GLOW
IN HEART PRAISE HIM
ACCEPT HIM
GET HIS
PEACE

I
WAKE UP
EACH MORNING
AND SEE ALL THE
BEAUTY HE HAS MADE
ALL AROUND US
HE GIVES LIFE
BLESSINGS
TOO

~PRAYING FOR YOU~
(SENRYU SUIT)

I'M PRAYING FOR YOU
YOU HAVE SO MUCH PAIN SORROWS
BUT THERE'S ALWAYS HOPE

IN CHRIST THERE'S TOMORROWS
JUST TRUST HIM AND TEST HIS WAYS
HE NEVER LEAVES YOU

HIS MERCY JUST SHOWS
IN HIM ALL IT IS POSSIBLE
IF YOU SEEK HIS LIGHT

NOW HEART BLEEDS FOR YOU
HOPING THAT YOU FIND YOUR WAY
EACH DAY FOR YOU PRAY

*

*

~CONTROL~
(FREE STYLE)

LEARN TO CONTROL YOURSELF AND YOU'LL BE FINE
LOSING CONTROL IS BAD, DENOTES LACK OF DISCIPLINE
YOU CAN'T CONTROL OTHERS BUT YOU CAN CONTROL THE SELF
WHY CONTROL OTHERS WHEN YOU CAN'T EVEN CONTROL YOURSELF

YOU CAN CONTROL MANY THINGS LIKE A REGULAR MACHINE
CONTROLLING PEOPLE, WELL THAT'S ANOTHER STORY
THERE ARE THINGS AND EVENTS THAT ARE OUT OF OUR HANDS
MAN CAN'T CONTROL NATURE, SO WHY TRY TO GET THAT GLORY

GIVING ADVICE IS GOOD TO GIVE TO OTHERS IF ASKED
BUT TRYING TO CONTROL EVERYTHING IS SIMPLY A MISTAKE
TRYING TO CONTROL OTHER LIVES IS JUST A FOOLISH DREAM
LACK OF CONTROL AND DISCIPLINE BRINGS ONLY HEARTACHE

BEHAVIOUR AND TEMPER YOU SHOULD CONTROL ALL THE TIME
WHEN YOU'RE OUT OF CONTROL YOU'RE NOT THINKING FINE
LACK OF JUDGMENT COMES FROM A MIND OUT OF CONTROL
PRACTICE SELF-CONTROL AND THEN YOUR LIFE WILL SHINE.

~FALL~
(A DOUBLE WHITNEY)

**FALL WILL BE
BACK SOON AND THE
TREES WILL LOSE
THEIR LEAVES AND CHANGE
WILL SEE NICE
COLORS AND HUES
IN YELLOWS BROWNS REDS AND GREENS**

**MUCH BEAUTY
FOR US TO SEE
AND ENJOY
DURING FALL MONTHS
CELEBRATE
AIR IS FRESH NICE
AFTER THE HOT SUMMER MONTHS**

*

*

~LABOR DAY 2012~
(SEDOKA)

TODAY'S LABOR DAY
HONOR AMERICAN WORKER
PRAISE THEM ALL FOR THEIR HARD WORK

THIS DAYS SET ASIDE
TO CHEER CELEBRATE WORKER'S
ACHIEVEMENTS IN ALL THAT THEY DO

*

*

~SUPERMAN~
(QUATRAINS)

**SUPERMAN HAS ALWAYS BEEN A SUPERHERO OF MINE
ONE OF MY FAVORITES OF ALL AND THAT WITH ME IS MORE THAN FINE.
SUPERMAN HE'S SO HANDSOME AND HE'S SO VERY COOL
HE CAN FLY!AND HE'S SO BRIGHT,SMART,AND HE'S NEVER A FOOL.**

**SUPERMAN IN HIS SUPERHERO OUTFIT LOOKS SO SHARP AND GOOD
AND FOR TRUTH AND JUSTICE FOR ANYONE ALWAYS PROUD STOOD
THERE'S NO ONE IN THE WORLD LIKE CHRISTOPHER REEVES AS SUPERMAN
SUPERMAN FIGHTS FOR EVERYTHING THAT STANDS FOR GOOD AND THAT'S HIS PLAN.**

**SUPERMAN,FIGHT FOR THE AMERICAN WAY AND HAS TONS OF DIE-HARD DEVOTED FANS
HE ALWAYS COMES SHINING THRU FOR ALL,EVIL IN ALL HIS FILMS HE BANS
SUPERMAN IN THE WORLD OF SUPERHEROES IS MY NUMBER ONE AND MANY OF US AGREED
NO OTHER SUPERHERO CAN EVER BEAT HIM WITH ALL ITS UNIQUE ATTRIBUTES INDEED.**

*

*

~YOU NEED TO~
(ITALIAN MADRIGAL)

YOU NEED KEEP DOOR OPEN'D TO LOVE
FORGIVE PAST HURTS, REACH FROM ABOVE
MEASURE TO HIS WORD, GOD IS LOVE.

YOU NEED KEEP DOOR OPEN'D TO LIFE
AT TIMES GET RID OF YOUR STRIFE
HIS PURE LOVE IS LARGER THAN LIFE

JUST DON'T GIVE UP ON LIFE BUT CLIMB
GOD MERCIFULLY WATCHES ALL TIME.

YOUR HEART TO LOVE JUST KEEP OPEN
HAVE FAITH! BELIEVE! GOD PAST HURTS MENDS.

*

*

~TODAY AND FOREVER~
(QUATERN)

**WITHOUT GOD DON'T KNOW WHERE I'D BE
HE SENDS BLESSINGS THAT'S CLEAR TO SEE
HE GIVES LOVE TODAY FOREVER
GRANTS FORGIVENESS AND LEAVES NEVER.**

**NO MATTER WHAT HE SEES THRU ALL
WITHOUT GOD DON'T KNOW WHERE I'D BE
THERE ARE DAYS IT'S HARD TO STAND TALL
HE SENDS BLESSINGS THAT'S CLEAR TO SEE.**

**NO MATTER WHAT HE SEES THRU ALL
WITH JESUS THRU THINGS I CAN GO
WITHOUT GOD DON'T KNOW WHERE I'D BE
WITH HIS DIVINE LOVE EACH DAY GROW.**

**HE GIVES LOVE TODAY FOREVER
HE SENDS BLESSINGS THAT'S CLEAR TO SEE
GRANTS FORGIVENESS AND LEAVES NEVER
WITHOUT GOD DON'T KNOW WHERE I'D BE.**

*

*

~AUTUMN DREAMER~
(SESTINA)

THERE ARE THOSE TIMES IN MY LIFE I DON'T REALLY KNOW ANYMORE WHAT I WANT
AND CONFUSED THERE ARE ALL THOSE EQUAL TIMES THAT I CAN'T SEE ANY LIGHT
MY HEART TELLS ME NOT TO GIVE UP AS I CONTINUE ON MY WAY LIKE THIS EVERY DAY
LIKE I'VE BEEN DOING ALL THIS TIME AND CONTINUE TO DO SO ONE WAY OR ANOTHER TOO
BECAUSE NOTHING SHOULD STOP ME FROM REACHING ANY OF MY GOALS DAY AND NIGHT
I KNOW IT WON'T BE EASY BUT THERE'S ALWAYS A WAY TO ACCOMPLISH WHAT I SEE

SO MANY THINGS I'VE ALREADY GONE THROUGH THIS LIFE SO FAR, SO MANY OF THEM ONLY GOD KNOWS YOU SEE
I DON'T REALLY SEE ANYTHING WRONG WITH WISHING AND DREAMING EVERYDAY OF ALL THE THINGS I WANT
RELEASING MY POOR CAPTURED HEART HERE AND NOW, DREAMING UNDER THE MOONLIGHT WHEN IT DELIVERS THE NIGHT
TRYING SO HARD DEEP INSIDE TO UNDERSTAND SO MANY THINGS I CAN'T SEE IN THE DARKNESS WITHOUT ANY LIGHT
IT'S SO VERY SAD FOR ME TO REALIZE THAT HARDLY NOTHING IS THE WAY I BELIEVE IT TO BE AT ONE POINT TOO
HAVE TO LEARN TO LIVE WITH THIS IN MY HEART AND SOUL, THERE'S NOTHING I CAN DO ABOUT THIS TODAY OR ANY DAY

AND THAT'S THE WAY THINGS ALWAYS WILL BE, AND HAVE TO ACCEPT THEM NO MATTER WHAT AS THEY COME EVERY DAY
SOMETIMES, THERE'S NOTHING I CAN DO ANYWAY, THERE'S SO MUCH I CAN DO ON MY OWN WITHOUT GOD I CAN SEE
I JUST WISH THAT EVERYTHING WAS A LITTLE EASIER TO DEAL WITH IN MY LIFE AND IN YOUR LIFE NATURALLY TOO
KNOWING SO WELL THAT WHAT I DREAM AND DESIRE CAN'T COME TRUE EVERY TIME THAT I WANT
THOUGHTS THAT COME AND GO CRASHING, FLYING,PIECES IN MY MIND LIKE CONFUSED PUZZLES THAT GLOW IN THE NIGHT

WONDERING MOST OF THE TIME WHAT HAVE I DONE SO WRONG? WHY ISN'T MORE LIGHT SHOWING IN THE HEART OF THE NIGHT
BLINDLY SURROUND IT BY ALL THIS DARKNESS MY SOUL PAUSES AND MAKES SURE I CAN SEE MY WAY AGAIN DURING THE DAY
AS I GROW WEARY BY THE DAILY ROUTINE, MY SOUL SLUMBERS TO REST TILL ANOTHER DAYLIGHT
AND THAT'S THE WAY THINGS WILL ALWAYS BE FOR ME NOW AND FOREVER I CAN SEE
HAVING LEARNED A LONG TIME THAT SOMETIMES IT DOESN'T REALLY

MATTER WHAT REALLY ONE MIGHT WANT
LET'S THEN MAKE THE BEST OF THIS JOURNEY IN WHICH BOTH TRAVELED ALREADY AS YOU KNOW THIS TOO

ONE WAY OR ANOTHER IN MY MIND AND SOUL I WILL SOMEWHAT SURVIVE ALL THIS TOO
BECAUSE THERE'S A MIGHTY POWER MUCH GREATER PROTECTING ME OUT THERE EVERY SINGLE DAY AND NIGHT
KNOWING THAT IN THE END IT'S ALL UP TO ME TO MAKE OF MY LIFE WHAT I CHOOSE IT TO BE OR I WANT
FOR ONE WAY OR ANOTHER NO MATTER WHAT TIME NEVER STOPS AND FROM NIGHT REVOLVS A NEW DAY
AND NOT ALL THAT YOU THINK OR YOU KNOW IT'S WHAT YOU REALLY BELIEVE- OR YOU SEE
AND AT THE END OF THE DAY IT COMES A TIME WHEN I HAVE TO FACE EACH ONE OF MY FEARS IN THE LIGHT

FOR LITTLE BY LITTLE THE SHADOWS RECEDE WHEN THEY MEET AND WELCOME THE LIGHT
MY SOUL STRETCHES BEYOND AND WHOLLY PARTAKES OF MY VIEW TOO
THINGS HAVE A WAY TO WORK FOR THE BEST ON WAY OR ANOTHER, DON'T YOU SEE?
IN THE DAYLIGHT WE CAN SEE BETTER THAN WHAT WE CAN'T SEE IN THE NIGHT
LET'S TRY TO MAKE THE VERY BEST OF WHAT WE CAN DO EVERY SINGLE DAY
BURNING THOUGHTS THAT I CAN'T CONTROL EVERY SINGLE TIME THAT I WANT

WHEN I SEE THE LIGHT I KNOW THEN THAT THE DARKNESS HAS GONE WITH THE NIGHT
AND FOR ME TOO THEN WILL BE A NEW SET OF HOPES WITH A BRAND-NEW DAY
'CAUSE AS FAR AS I CAN SEE AND I KNOW I CAN DO WITH MY LIFE WHAT I WANT.

*

~MY CAT~
(TRIPLE QUATRAINS)

I JUST LOVE VERY MUCH MY CAT
TWINKLE IS HER NAME YOU MAY KNOW THAT
NO MATTER IF I PREFER DOGS
TWINKLE I LOVE THOUGH I LIKE MORE DOGS.

TWINKLE IS THE BEST CAT TO ME
SHE MAKES ME LAUGH AND JUST GLEE
OF MY HEART SHE HOLDS THE KEY
AND NOW KNOW SHE HAS NO FLEAS.

ALL THE TIME TWINKLE WASHES HERSELF UP
SHE'S MUCH BIGGER THAN AN AVERAGE CUP
SHE GRACES EVERYDAY MY HOME
AND STAYS ROUND,AND LOTS SHE ROAMS.

~ONLY WITH YOU~
(PANTOUM)

THIS IS WHERE NOW I AM WITH YOU
NOW JUST WANT TO BE WITH YOU TOO
FELL DEEPLY IN LOVE JUST LOVE YOU
I JUST BELIEVE YOUR LOVE IS TRUE.

NOW I JUST WANT TO BE WITH YOU
SO MANY THINGS HAD MADE US BLUE
I JUST DO KNOW YOUR LOVE IS TRUE
WE'VE GONE THRU SO MUCH THAT TOO

SO MANY THINGS HAD MADE US BLUE
WITH YOU ALWAYS MY HEART CAN DANCE
WE'VE GONE THRU SO MUCH THAT TOO
BUT MORE THAN HAPPY I TAKE CHANCE

WITH YOU ALWAYS MY HEART CAN DANCE
FELL DEEPLY IN LOVE JUST LOVE YOU
BUT MORE THAN HAPPY I TAKE CHANCE
THIS IS WHERE NOW I AM WITH YOU.

*

*

~NOT ENOUGH TIME~
(SONNET)

THEY SAY SHE HAD EVERYTHING TO LIVE FOR
DID SHE?PERHAPS,IF SHE WOULD HAD TIME MORE
BUT IN THE END THAT WASN'T JUST MEANT TO BE
SHE WAS BEAUTIFUL,LIKE A ROSE,ALONE.
HER MERE PRESENCE LIKE A STAR ALWAYS SHONE
YET, LIKE STAR FROM HEAVEN ONE NIGHT WAS GONE
SHE FELL.HER BEAUTY 'MONG MORTALS WAS LOST
STILL,SHE WALKS THIS EARTH WITH GRACEFULNESS MOST
DEATH!O DEATH!WITH HIS FATAL KISS TOOK HER 'WAY
DEATH HAD HIS WAY WHEN FOR HER CAME THAT DAY
SHE SEEM'D HAD IT ALL,BUT,TIME SHE HAD NOT
THAT,STILL SHE HAD EVERYTHING TO LIVE FOR
PERHAPS SHE DID,WONDER IF JUST HAD MORE
TIME,BUT THAT WAS SOMETHING SHE HAD MORE NOT.

~SUNRISE~
(QUATRAINS)

WHEN THE SUNRISE SLOWLY CREEPS IN
ALL THE SHADOWS START TO GROW SHORT
THEN ALL OF SUDDEN A BRAND-NEW DAYS IN
NOW IS TIME TO DO THINGS OF ALL SORTS.

AND WHEN THE SUN COMES OUT EVERY DAY
IT JUST COMES FOR AWHILE ANYWAY
HIDING WITH IT SOME MISTERY YEA,
AS DAY PROGRESSES YOU WORK AND PLAY.

AND SURELY ENOUGH THE HOURS WILL FLEE
WHEN SUNRISE IN THE HORIZON CREEPS IN
IN THE AIR HEAR SOUND OF SIGHS AND GLEE
THEN ALL OF SUDDEN A BRAND-NEW DAYS IN.

*

*

~LIKE ANY DAY~
(PANTOUM)

DAYS NOT LOOKING BAD AND OF THIS I'M GLAD
I WON'T LET ANYTHING MAKE ME BLUE/MAD
AS I TAKE CARE OF ALL I NEED TO DO
TODAY MUCH TO ACCOMPLISH OLD AND NEW.

I WON'T LET ANYTHING MAKE ME BLUE/MAD
AND LIKE ANY DAY I'LL PRAY MAKE IT THRU
TODAY MUCH TO ACCOMPLISH OLD AND NEW
FOR WITH GOD ANYTHING GOOD CAN COME TRUE.

AND LIKE ANY DAY I'LL PRAY MAKE IT THRU
I'LL HAVE MY BEST ATTITUDE AND NICE SMILE
FOR WITH GOD ANYTHING GOOD CAN COME TRUE
AND WITH HIS HELP I CAN RUN ALL MY MILES.

I'LL HAVE MY BEST ATTITUDE AND NICE SMILE
AS I TAKE CARE OF ALL I NEED TO DO
AND WITH HIS HELP I CAN RUN ALL MY MILES
DAY NOT LOOKING BAD AND OF THIS I'M GLAD.

*

*

~WORRIES~
(CHANT)

WORRIES,WORRIES, MORE TODAY
WORRIES,WORRIES,SEND THEM AWAY
WORRIES,WORRIES, DON'T FRET FRIEND
WORRIES,WORRIES! GOD HELP WILL SEND
WORRIES,WORRIES, DO YOU CARE?
WORRIES,WORRIES, SOME I CAN'T BEAR
WORRIES,WORRIES,TOSS AWAY
WORRIES,WORRIES, HAVE THEM EACH DAY.

*

~FOR SO LONG~
(SONNET)

HOW I LONG FOR DAYS WHEN MY HEART WAS FREE
WHEN OFTEN DREAMS BROUGHT LOTS OF SMILES AND GLEE
REMEMBER TODAY ALL YOUR KISSES AGAIN
WITH EXCITEMENT THAT ALWAYS DWELLS IN.
HOLDING MY PEN I'M READY AGAIN TO WRITE,
SAY BYE TO THIS DAY AND WELCOMED THE NIGHT.
TELL ME HOW COULD I EVER BE SO WRONG?
WHEN I'VE LOVED YOU WITH PASSION FOR SO LONG
HOPE AND DEVOTION PIECES CHARDS OF MY HEART
BUT WITH EACH BEAT YOU TAKE IT ALL APART.
AND TIME SEEMS TO STAND ALL OF SUDDEN STILL
WITH CRAFTY WORDS AND LIES,LOVE,TURNS HEARTS ILL.
HOW I LONG FOR DAYS CARE-FREE OF YOUTH WHEN
WE WALK'D SO IN LOVE HAND IN HAND,BACK THEN.

*

*

~MORNING SALUTATIONS~
(LAI)

SUNR'SE SOFTLY SOARS IN
GREETS ALL WITH A GRIN.
BELLS RING
FOLKS GET OUT,GO IN
THE SUNS A TAD DIN
KIDS SING
MAKING NOTES WITH PINS
LOVE BIRDS SWEET SONGS IN
HEARTS BRINGS.

~JUST WHEN~
(MODIFIED PANTOUM)

WHEN THE SUNRISE SLOWLY CREEPS IN
AND ALL OF SUDD'N NEW DAY BEGINS
WHEN THE SHADOWS START TO GROW SHORT
TIME TO DO THINGS AND BE GOOD SPORT.

WHEN THE SHADOWS START TO GROW SHORT
WHEN THE BRIGHT SUN COMES OUT EACH DAY
TIME TO DO THINGS AND BE A SPORT
AS DAY PROGRESSES WORK AND PLAY.

WHEN THE BRIGHT SUN COMES OUT EACH DAY
IT HIDES LOTS OF MYSTERIES YEA
AS DAY PROGRESSES WORK AND PLAY
IT JUST COMES FOR AWHILE ANY WAY.

IT HIDES LOTS OF MYSTERIES YEA
WHEN THE SHADOWS START TO GROW SHORT
IT JUST COMES FOR AWHILE ANY WAY
WHEN THE SUNRISE SLOWLY CREEPS IN.

*

*

~CHRISTMAS~
(CHANT)

CHRISTMAS,CHRISTMAS,ENJOY DAY
CHRISTMAS,CHRISTMAS,HAPPY NOT BLUE
CHRISTMAS,CHRISTMAS,CHRISTMAS HERE
CHRISTMAS,CHRISTMAS,IT BRINGS US CHEER
CHRISTMAS,CHRISTMAS,TIME FULL OF JOY
CHRISTMAS,CHRISTMAS,SOME GET GIFTS,TOYS
CHRISTMAS,CHRISTMAS,GOD CHILD IS BORN
CHRISTMAS,CHRISTMAS,TODAY THIS MORN!

*

*

*

~TODAY AND FOREVER~
(QUATERN)

WITHOUT GOD DON'T KNOW WHERE I'D BE
HE SENDS BLESSINGS THAT'S CLEAR TO SEE
HE GIVES LOVE TODAY FOREVER
GRANTS FORGIVENESS AND LEAVES NEVER.

NO MATTER WHAT HE SEES THRU ALL
WITHOUT GOD DON'T KNOW WHERE I'D BE
THERE ARE DAYS IT'S HARD TO STAND TALL
HE SENDS BLESSINGS THAT'S CLEAR TO SEE.

NO MATTER WHAT HE SEES THRU ALL
WITH JESUS THRU THINGS I CAN GO
WITHOUT GOD DON'T KNOW WHERE I'D BE
WITH HIS DIVINE LOVE EACH DAY GROW.

HE GIVES LOVE TODAY FOREVER
HE SENDS BLESSINGS THAT'S CLEAR TO SEE
GRANTS FORGIVENESS AND LEAVES NEVER
WITHOUT GOD DON'T KNOW WHERE I'D BE.

*

*

*

~TWINKLE~
(QUATRAIN)

TWINKLE IS THE NAME OF OUR PET CAT
SHE'S BEAUTIFUL CAT WHO DOESN'T LIKE A HAT
STILL TWINKLE IS A PURE LADY ALL THE WAY THRU
SHE SLEEPS A LOT AND LOVES TO PLAY WITH YOU.

TWINKLE LIKES HER FILLED BOWL OF MEAL
SHE NEVER EVER FOR FOOD NEEDS TO STEAL
BUT LIKE THERMOSTAT HER MOOD CHANGES HUE
AND SHE PICKS FIGHTS WITH OTHERS CATS TOO.

IF SHE HAPPENS TO SEE OTHER CATS AROUND
SHE CHASES THEM POOR THINGS TILL NO ONE IS FOUND
WE ALL LOVE THAT TWINKLE SO MUCH SO VERY DEAR
BUT SHE CAN BE A HANDFUL AT TIMES BE FAR OR NEAR.

SHE'S BRAVE BUT AT TIMES SHE CAN BE LIKE ANOTHER SCARY CAT
WATCHING HER MOODS SHE ENJOYS TO TEASE THEN SHE JUST SCATS
AND WHEN SOMEONE PETS HER SHE JUST MOVES WILDLY HER TAIL
THAT TWINKLE FOR SURE CAN PUT YOU IN A BOX WITH A NAIL.

TWINKLE LOVES TO ROLL UPON THE DIRT TOO
SHE GETS HER SHARE OF FOOD AND MUCH MORE THAN IS DUE
SHE DEMANDS HER SHARE OF MILK AND MORE THAN A LITTLE TOO
TWINKLE IS A GREAT PET FOR SURE, SHE BRINGS US LOTS OF FUN.

~MY LOVE~
(PANTOUM)

**MY LOVE YOU MAY CALL ME DAY AND NIGHT
BECAUSE I THINK OF YOU ANYWAY, ALL DAY LONG
I CANNOT LIVE WITHOUT YOU DAY OR NIGHT
AND IN THIS I DON'T SEE ANYTHING WRONG**

**BECAUSE I THINK OF YOU ANYWAY ALL DAY LONG
YOU MAY WANT TO CALL ME ANY TIME YOU WANT
AND IN THIS I DON'T SEE ANYTHING WRONG
LIVING WITHOUT YOUR LOVE I CAN'T**

**YOU MAY WANT TO CALL ME ANY TIME YOU WANT
DO IT NIGHT AND DAY ALL THE TIME
LIVING WITHOUT YOUR LOVE I CAN'T
AND INTO ETERNITY WE CAN SING AND WITH LOVE RHYME**

**DO IT NIGHT AND DAY ALL THE TIME
I CANNOT LIVE WITHOUT YOU DAY OR NIGHT
AND INTO ETERNITY WE CAN SING AND WITH LOVE RHYME
MY LOVE YOU MAY CALL ME DAY AND NIGHT.**

~CHRISTMAS COMES WITH LOVE~
(TANKA SUIT)

I BOUGHT THIS FOR YOU
AND I WANT YOU KNOW TODAY
HOW MUCH I LOVE YOU
IT'S GIVEN WITH ALL MY HEART
CELEBRATE JESUS WE DO.

CHRISTMAS CAN BE FUN
MAKE BEST OF THE TIME WE GOT
AFTER ALL IS DONE
WE CAN SING AND DANCE A LOT
EXCITEMENT IN ALL JUST SHOWN.

SOME SNOW STARTS TO FALL
CHRISTMAS TREES GLISTENS WITH LIGHTS
BY NOW GONE IS FALL
STARS SHINE SHIMMERING THE NIGHTS
FOLKS SHOP CROWDING ALL THE MALLS.

CHILDREN LAUGH PLAYING
OUTSIDE WHILE SNOWMAN BUILDING
HANG ORNAMENTS ON TREE
LOTS OF SMILES JESUS IS THE KEY
CHILDREN HAPPY WHEN TOYS SEE.

*

*

*

~HAMSTERS~
(QUATRAINS)

**HAMSTERS ARE SO CUTE
THEY CAN GET IN YOUR BOOT
MAKE A WONDERFUL PET
DON'T HAVE TO RUN IN DEBT.**

**HAMSTERS ARE VERY FURRY
ALWAYS RUNNING IN A HURRY
THEY ALL FIT IN YOUR HAND
AND CAN LOOK NICE AND GRAND.**

**HAMSTERS IN THE PAST I'VE HAD
THEY CAN BITE YET THEY'RE NOT BAD
HAMSTERS ARE SO VERY SMALL
HOLD THEM FAST OR THEY WILL FALL.**

*

*

~WITHOUT GOD~
(PANTOUM)

WITHOUT GOD,I DON'T KNOW WHERE NOW I'D BE
HE SENDS ME HIS BLESSINGS THAT'S CLEAR TO SEE
HE GIVES HIS LOVE TODAY AND FOREVER
HE GRANTS FORGIVENESS,HE ABANDONS NEVER.

HE SENDS ME HIS BLESSINGS THAT'S CLEAR TO SEE
NO MATTER WHAT HE ALWAYS SEES THROUGH ALL
HE GRANTS FORGIVENESS,HE ABANDONS NEVER
THERE ARE DAYS WHEN IT'S SO HARD TO STAND TALL.

NO MATTER WHAT HE ALWAYS SEES THROUGH ALL
WITH JESUS BY SIDE THROUGH ALL I CAN GO
THERE ARE DAYS WHEN IT'S SO HARD TO STAND TALL
BUT HIS LOVE AND GRACE HELPS ME EACH DAY GROW.

~YOUR LOVE~
(DOUBLE TANKA)

I CAN SEE YOUR LOVE
IN ALL THAT YOU DO FOR ME
YOUR DEAR FACE I SEE
YOUR LOVE EACH DAY I CAN TOUCH
I'M SO HAPPY YOU'RE WITH ME

YOU'RE SO FINE TO ME
AND YOU'RE SO BEAUTIFUL TOO
LET'S GET TOGETHER
WE CAN HAVE FUN FOREVER
SO COME JOIN ME AND YOU'LL SEE.

*

*

~TIME IMPORTANT TO US ALL DAY LONG~
(A GHAZAL)

TIMES IMPORTANT TO US ALL DAY LONG
LIFE IS TOO SHORT AND IT WON'T LAST LONG.

DREAM,TAKE A LOOK,THINGS CAN GET BETTER
CHRISTMAS IS ON ITS WAY, WON'T BE LONG.

A JOYOUS HEART, A YAWN, AND A SIGH...
CAN'T DO IT ALL, BUT TRY ALL DAY LONG.

LIFE IS UNPREDICTABLE THATS A FACT
WEAR A SMILE, DO YOUR BEST ALL LIFE LONG.

SOME CHOICES ARE YOURS TO MAKE DORIAN
ENJOY LIFE FOR GOOD TIMES WON'T LAST LONG.

*

*

*

~ANOTHER MORNING EMBRACES THE DAY~
(RONDEAU)

ANOTHER MORNING, EMBRACES THE DAY
AS I GRAB MY CUP OF COFFEE, AND I AM ON MY WAY,
OUTSIDE I HEAR FLYCATCHERS SING,
AND WATCH THE BUTTERFLIES TAKE A LITTLE SPIN,
SURROUNDED, BY SCENTED ROSES OF MANY ARRAYS.

SITTING ACROSS,A LAKE OF BLUE IN COMPLETE REPOSE
WARM SUNSHINE KISSES AND CARESSES ALL MY NOSE,
AND SENDS OH, SO FAST, ALL MY CARES AWAY
ANOTHER MORNING.

TRYING TO STEAL HERE AN EARLY BREAK,
CATCHING ME A WEE NAP, LIKE IT, EVERY WEEK,
TO THINK AND GET MY POOR MIND IN TOUCH,ORGANIZE
SIPPING ANOTHER CUP OF COFFEE IS A GOD-SENT PRIZE
AS I TOTALLY EMBRACE THE DAY, AND TAKE ANOTHER PEEK,
ANOTHER MORNING.

*

*

~TODAY~
(SONNET)

**DAY LOOKING NOT BAD AND OF THIS I'M GLAD
AS I TAKE CARE OF ALL I NEED TO DO
TODAY MUCH TO ACCOMPLISH OLD AND NEW
SOME THINGS NOT MUCH DIFFERENT I MUST ADD
I WON'T LET ANYTHING MAKE ME BLUE/MAD
AND LIKE ANY DAY I PRAY MAKE IT THRU
FOR WITH GOD ANYTHING GOOD WILL COME TRUE
AS I GO THRU DAY TURNS HAPPY OR SAD.**

**I'LL JUST PUT ON MY BEST FACE AND NICE SMILE
IN BAD WEATHER I'LL DO BEST ALL THE WHILE
TOSS TO WIND WORRIES DELETE BAD PAST FILES
AND WITH GOD'S HELP I CAN RUN ALL MY MILES.**

**TODAY SO FAR IT'S BEEN A V'RY GOOD DAY.
TO GOD I PRAY IT CONTINUES THIS WAY.**

*

*

~AUTUMN BLESSINGS~
(BLESSED HEART)

FEEL CHILL IN THE****AIR EVERYWHERE**
FALL IS WONDERFUL*** AND YOU CAN HAVE FUN**
CAUSE IN SO MANY WAYS IS DIFFERENT FROM
THE OTHER THREE SEASONS AND THERES JUST NONE
LIKE FALL YOU CAN SEE THE TREES CHANGING
COLOURS AS THEY SHOW BEAUTIFUL HUES
SOMETIMES YOU CAN SMELL CINNAMON
WHICH LINGERS ON THE AIR WITH
PUMPKIN PIE IN THE MIX
CHILDREN HAVE FUN
PLAY WITH LEAVES
THAT COVERS
GROUND

*

*

~IT GROWS~
(MY STYLE)

HOPE GROWS
IN HEART THAT'S SO
WITHING ME THERE'S A SONG
I'VE WAITED FOR THIS FOR SO LONG
MY HEART THE LORD KNOWS IT SO WELL
LOVE FOR HIM HE CAN ALWAYS TELL
I'VE WAITED FOR THIS SO LONG
WITHIN ME THERE'S A SONG
IN HEART THAT'S SO
HOPE GROWS.

*

*

~TWO PICTURES~
(MINI GLOSA)

TEXT:

TWO PICTURES ON AN ANCIENT WALL
IN THE GRAND FLORENTINE HALL

ANONYMOUS

TWO PICTURES ON AN ANCIENT WALL.
ONE SHOWS A FAIR GIRL WHO LOOKS LIKE A DOLL.
THIS PICTURE IS VERY OLD AND KIND OF TALL,
THE OTHER ONE IN COMPARISON IT'S NOT THAT SMALL.
MULTITUDES ATTEND NOW THIS ART SHOW,HAVE A BALL.
TWO PICTURES ON AN ANCIENT WALL.

IN THE GRAND FLORENTINE HALL.
IT ATTRACTS AND FASCINATES THE EYES OF ALL.
THE OTHER PAINTING SHOWING THE YOUNG MAN IS FINE.
HE SHOWS MAGNIFICENTLY IN HIS ANCESTRAL CASTLE SCENE.
BOTH PAINTINGS HANG NOW SIDE BY SIDE
IN THE GRAND FLORENTINE HALL.

~YEARNINGS~
(DOUBLE SENRYU)

DAY QUICKLY SHRIVELS IN
DARK WHISPERS,AS LIGHT DEPARTS
TAKING MUCH WITH IT

DREAMS CONJURE MEMORIES
IN THIS COLD ROOM WITHOUT YOU
YEARNING YOUR TOUCH AGAIN

*

*

*

\

~CHILDREN~
(THE CHANT)

CHILDREN, CHILDREN, RING THE BELL
CHILDREN, CHILDREN, STUDY THIS SO WELL
CHILDREN, CHILDREN, JUST BEHAVE
CHILDREN, CHILDREN, JUST BE SO BRAVE
CHILDREN, CHILDREN, PLAY THE GAME
CHILDREN, CHILDREN, JUST DO THE SAME
CHILDREN, CHILDREN, DO AS TOLD
CHILDREN, CHILDREN, RING 'GAIN THE BELL!

IN A DAY LIKE TODAY~
(SONNET)

**FOR WINTER,KIND OF COOL HERE,YES,IT WAS
VERY NICE TODAY,COMPLETED QUITE SOME,A BIT
THEN JUST RELAXED,REFLECTED 'LONG,DID SIT
AFTER MANY CHORES I'VE DONE,TOOK A PAUSE
READ IN 1927 DR.SEUSS MARRI'D HELEN PALMER
IN 1927, KING TUT'S TOMB WAS DISCOVERED TOO
MANY EVENTS IN A DAY LIKE TODAY
BEFELL.SOME GOOD,SOME BAD,CATCHY SCAR OR STAR.**

**TURN OFF TV.ONLY DEPRESSING,JOYLESS SHOWS
TODAY,WRITING HERE ANOTHER NEW SONNET
NOW,AGAIN,FOR A THIRD DAY IN A ROW
MULLING OVER,JUST SURFING ROUND THE NET.**

**IN 1877,EDISON HIS CRANK'D PHONOGRAPH PLAY'D
IN 1981,FAMED,ACTRESS NATALIE WOOD DIED.**

*

~TOMORROW~
(QUATERN)

YESTERDAY JUST CAME AND LEFT AGAIN
AND NOW IT SEEMS JUST LIKE A DREAM
IT'LL BE MEMORY IN MY BRAIN
THAT MAY BRING SUNSHINES HAPPY GLEAM.

I JUST TRY TO ENJOY'D WHAT I'VE GOT
YESTERDAY JUST CAME AND LEFT AGAIN
THINK I CAN MAKE IT ON THE DOT
I KNOW THE EFFORT ISN'T IN VAIN.

IF I CAN ONLY FOLLOW GODS PLAN
AND DON'T GET STUCK IN THE PAST
YESTERDAY JUST CAME AND LEFT AGAIN
WITH ALL ITS UPS AND DOWNS FAST.

EVERYTHING HAS ITS BAD GOOD DAYS
NOW LEFT HOLDING MORE MEMORIES
BUT 'MORROW SUNSHINE JUST HOPES RAISES
YESTERDAY JUST CAME AND LEFT AGAIN

~WORDS~
(CHANT)

WORDS,WORDS, I ENJOY EACH DAY
WORDS,WORDS,THAT IN HEART AND MIND STAY.
WORDS,WORDS,JUST TAKE ANOTHER LOOK
WORDS,WORDS, THAT LIVE IN THE GOOD BOOK.
WORDS,WORDS,OH MY!THEY'RE SO COOL!
WORDS,WORDS,WE ALL LEARN IN A SCHOOL.
WORDS,WORDS,THEY'RE ALWAYS GREAT TOOL.
WORDS,WORDS,I JUST ENJOY EACH DAY.

*

~FAITH~
(QUATRAIN)

**FAITH IN JESUS MAKES IT ALL POSSIBLE,
TO STAND STRONGER WHEN MY FLESH IS WEAK,
HE'S ALWAYS THERE WHEN I NEED A FRIEND
HIS LOVE NEVER CHANGES OR TAKES A BREAK.**

**SAFE WITH HIM BEYOND ANY WORLDLY HARM,
OH JESUS! YOU'RE THE SOURCE OF ALL MY LIGHT,
HE TELLS ME TO TRUST HIM EVERYDAY IN LIFE
AND HOW TO START EACH AND EVERY DAY AND NIGHT**

**I CLAIM WITH ALL MY HEART AND SOUL
HIS HOLY AND BLESSED NAME FOREVER,WITH HIM I'M JUST FREE.
HE'S MY LIGHTHOUSE AND MY SOLID ROCK,
IN A STORM, HE GUIDES ME SAFELY ACROSS THE SHORES, YOU SEE.**

*

*

~HAPPY THANKSGIVING DAY WISHES TO YOU~
(HOTAN)

TODAY IS THANKSGIVING
A NICE DAY TO CELEBRATE
BE AROUND FAMILY AND FRIENDS
HAVE GOOD TIME
ENJOY A NICE MEAL
TALK AND LAUGH
TIME TO GET CLOSER
TO THANK GOD FOR EVERYTHING
RECALL HIS BLESSINGS

~BECAUSE HE CARES~
(MATHNAWI)

BELIEVERS KNOW THAT LIFE NEVER ENDS.IT'S SO!
CAUSE CHOOSE BELIEVE THERE'S A GOD AND LIFE JUST FLOWS.

IT'S GOOD FOR ME TO REALLY JUST BELIEVE
THAT THERE'S ETERNAL LIFE AFTER THIS EARTH WE LEAVE.

GOD IN HIS MERCY GIVES EVERYONE OPTION
DON'T CARE WHAT WORLD SAYS, I ACCEPT GOD. I'M ON!

FOR ME GODS FIRST, SIMPLE! HE'S MY COMFORTER
LIVING UNDER HIS LIGHT & GRACE IS GREAT. HE CARES.

*

*

~BROKEN DREAMS~
(ALLITERATION/RHYMING COUPLETS)

**SHARP LIGHT FALLS ANGRILY,
BALEFUL SUMMER ENTOMBS BLEAKLY,
AS CONCRETE VESSEL SIGHS COMPLETELY,
AND VIBRANT LIFE CRASHES HYPOCRITICALLY**

**UNIFORM DREAMS CRAVES CARESSINGLY,
TRIBAL BATTLE-AXE STOOPS SUGGESTIVELY,
AS VESTIGAL COMA CRASHES DAZZLINGLY,
AND A BROKEN LIGHT LANGUISHES SLEEPLESSLY**

**BROKEN DREAMS SHRIEKS CARESSINGLY,
GRAY COMA NAGS UNCOMFORTABLY;
AS DELIBERATE CREATIONISM DIES EXPECTANTLY,
AND SOUNDLESS ENTICEMENT CAPITULATES FINALLY**

*

*

~STAY FOCUS~
(FREE STYLE)

STAY FOCUS TILL YOU REACH YOUR GOALS
TAKE IT SLOW AND DO IT JUST ONE DAY AT A TIME
DON'T RUSH ON AND YOU'LL COMPLETE THE JOB JUST FINE
EVEN IF YOU DO IT FROM THE BOTTOM WHEN YOU CLIMB

DON'T EVER LOSE YOUR SIGHTS AND NEVER GIVE UP
JUST STAY FOCUS WITH ALL YOUR HEART AND YOUR MIND
KEEP YOUR FAITH AND HOPES TILL YOUR ACHIEVE YOUR DREAMS
DON'T EVER LET THEM GO OR JUST TOSS THEM IN THE WIND

KEEP YOUR HEART AND MIND ALL THE TIME FOCUS IN GOD
CHALLENGES AND PROBLEMS EVERYDAY WE KNOW ARISE
BUT AS LONG AS YOU STAY FOCUS ON YOUR GOALS AND HE
YOU'LL BE MORE THAN FINE AND WITH HIM MORE WISE.

~MOVIES THAT WE SEE~
(FREE STYLE)

MOVIES THAT WE SEE
GIVE US EXCITING HIGHS
ROMANCE, HORROR,THRILLS
MA'TER NOT HOW GOOD, BAD BE.

ENTERTAIN US DO
YES THIS DO ALL THE TIME
LEAVING THOUGHTS AWRY
IN VARIED WAYS AND THAT'S FINE.

IN LORD OF THE RINGS
DESOLATION,VALOR SEEN.
PRIDE & PREJUDICE'S GREAT
TOO,THEY'RE JUST LIKE FINE WINE.

MOVIES DO WE SEE
MA'TER NOT HOW GOOD, BAD BE.

*

*

*

~HAPPY THANKSGIVING DAY 2011~
(FREE STYLE)

WE THANK YOU GOD FOR OUR PLENTIFUL BOUNTY
FOR ALL THOSE IN LIFE WE LOVE AND SHARE
FOR ALL THE GOODNESS WE FARE SO WELL
FOR HIS LOVING PRESENCE THAT'S ALWAYS THERE.

WE OFFER THE BEST OF OURSELVES ON THIS DAY
OUR LOVE AND BLESSING MIXED WITH PRAISES AND A PRAY
IN EVERY WAY AND SHAPE FROM THE HEART TO DISPLAY
AS WE SIT DOWN LAVISHLY TO EAT TOGETHER ON THIS DAY.

TABLE FILLED TO THE VERY TOP
WITH TURKEY PUDDINGS AND GOODIES GALORE
ENJOY NOW A HOT AND FRESH CUP OF COFEE
AND A PIECE OF THE SWEETEST PUMPKIN PIE.

LET'S THANK GOD FOR ALL OUR WONDROUS BOUNTY
NOT JUST TODAY BUT LET'S DO IT EVERYDAY
LET'S THANK HIM WITH A PRAYER AND PRAISES ENDLESLY
FOR ALL THE LOVE AND THE LIFE THAT WE HAVE.

*

*

About the Author

Dorian Petersen Potter has been writing poetry for most of her life. Her poetry has been published in many anthologies and poetry collections all over the world. Her poetry today can be found in many places in the internet and in several of her poetry pages too.

Dorian's personal websites:

"Poetic Dreams"

http://www.PoetryPoem.com/ladydp2000

and

http://publishing with passion.com/dorianpetersenpotter.html

www.ingramcontent.com/pod-product-compliance
Ingram Content Group UK Ltd.
Pitfield, Milton Keynes, MK11 3LW, UK
UKHW041914190726
13854UKWH00003B/1242

9 781300 294368